REALLY
dirty
JOKES

summersdale

REALLY DIRTY JOKES

Copyright © Summersdale Publishers Ltd, 2007

Additional text by Anne-Sophie Perrin and Lucy York

All rights reserved.

Summersdale Publishers Ltd
46 West Street
Chichester
West Sussex
PO19 1RP
UK

www.summersdale.com

Printed and bound in Great Britain

ISBN: 1-84024-618-9

ISBN 13: 978-1-84024-618-6

REALLY

dirty

JOKES

SID FINCH

Three old ladies were resting their aching joints on a park bench when a man jumped out from behind a bush, flashed them and ran off. Two of them had a stroke, but the third was too slow.

A teenaged couple are feeling horny and go back to the boy's house for a night of steamy passion. Before they go upstairs, the boy says to the girl, 'By the way, I still share a room with my little brother, but he won't see us because I sleep on the top bunk. We'll have to whisper to each other in code though, so if you want me to go faster say "bread" and if you want me to slow down say "butter".' The girl agrees and

6

they get into bed and start
going for it, with the girl calling
out "bread" and then "butter"
every few minutes. Just as the
boy climaxes, his little brother
calls out, 'Can you two go
and make your sandwiches
in the kitchen? You're getting
mayonnaise all over me!'

How did the armless
man do in the wanking
competition?

He came nowhere.

There were two eggs boiling in a pan. One egg said to the other: 'Oh look, I've got a crack.' The other replied, 'Well there's no point telling me: I'm not hard yet!'

REALLY dirty JOKES

A woman was bored at home while her husband was away on business and decided to visit a fortune teller who had travelled to the area. The fortune teller immediately guessed that this woman was sexually frustrated and produced a jar which contained a pickled penis. 'If you want a good time,' she explained, 'all you have to do is unscrew the lid and say "Pickled penis: my vagina".' The woman paid up and took the penis home. That night she gave it a try and found that it worked, with fantastic results. She was moaning with pleasure when her husband arrived home, banged on the bedroom door and demanded to know who she had in there with her. 'It's OK darling,' she said, 'It's just my pickled penis.' As he burst through the door, her husband shouted, 'Pickled penis my ass!'

How do you get four
grannies to scream
'Oh FUCK!'?

Get another granny
to shout 'BINGO!'

It was a chilly winter night and two bulls were shivering in the farmer's field. One bull said to the other: 'Gosh it's cold!' 'Yes, it is,' agreed the other bull. 'You know, I might just go and slip into a nice Jersey.'

An American college graduate was travelling in Europe and met a beautiful blonde Swedish girl. He asked her out, and while they were dancing, he put his arms around her and said, 'In America, we call this a hug.' She replied, 'Yaah, we are also calling it a hug in Sveden.' So far so good, he thought, and decided to try for a French kiss. He said, 'In the States, we call this a kiss.' She replied, 'Yaah, in Sveden

also, this is a kiss.' They had a
couple more drinks and then
he suggested they go outside.
Finding a nice quiet spot in a
nearby park, he undressed her
and they started to have sex.
He said, 'In America, we call this
a grass sandwich.' She replied,
'Yaaah, in Sveden we call it
grass sandwich too, but usually
we are putting more meat in it.'

really dirty JOKES

What do train sets and boobs have in common?

Both were designed for kids, but it's always dads who end up playing with them.

A woman went to see her gynaecologist and complained of a sore vagina. During the examination, the doctor found a small vibrator stuck inside her. 'Ah,' he said, 'I think I can see what's causing your discomfort, but I'm afraid that removing the er… obstruction requires a lengthy, delicate and expensive surgical operation.' 'Well,' said the woman, 'I don't think I can afford it right now. As I'm here though, could you replace the batteries?'

John was showing off his new
sports car to his girlfriend.
'If I can get up to 200 mph,
will you strip off?' he asked.
'OK!' she agreed. He revved
the engine and before long
the car was speeding along at
200 mph. True to her word,
his girlfriend got completely
naked. John couldn't keep his
eyes on the road, and the car
skidded onto a grassy verge
and flipped over. His naked
girlfriend was thrown out of
the car and landed unscathed,

but John was trapped beneath the steering wheel. 'Get help!' he shouted. 'But I haven't got any clothes on and the doors are jammed shut!' 'Here, take my shoe to cover yourself,' said John. With the shoe held over her pubes, the girl ran to the nearest petrol station and said to the attendant, 'You have to help me – my boyfriend's stuck!' Looking at the shoe, the pump assistant said, 'I don't think there's anything I can do – looks like he's in too far.'

REALLY
dirty
JOKES

How do you know
that a mechanic's
been having sex?

He's got a clean finger.

An armless and legless cripple knocks at the door of a brothel. The doorman opens up and asks, 'What do you want, stumpy?' The cripple replies, 'Isn't that obvious? What do you think I knocked with?!'

On his first day working for a local paper, a young journalist is sent out to find a human-interest story. Driving through the countryside, he pulls over to talk to the first man he sees, introduces himself and asks, 'Living out here, has any event made you particularly happy?' After a moment's thought the man replies, 'Oh yes — once my neighbour's daughter got lost, so we set up a search party and found her. When we'd all shagged her, we took her home.' Somewhat taken aback, the naive reporter asks, 'Has anything else happened?' The man replies, 'Well, when one of my neighbour's pigs ran off, we found it and all…' 'I can't print that!' The reporter interrupts. 'What about an event that has made you particularly sad?' Hanging his head, the man replies, 'Well, there was this one time when I got lost…'

REALLY
dirty
JOKES

How can you tell
when a blonde's been
using a vibrator?

Her front teeth
are broken.

REALLY
dirty
JOKES

Two inflatable dolls
are walking through
the desert. Suddenly,
the first doll shouts
out to the second one,
'Watch out for the
CACTUSSSSSSsssssss...'

A traditional dairy farmer decides it's time to move with the times and invests in an automatic milking machine. On the day it arrives, his wife is away at market and he can't resist the temptation to try it out on himself. After a frustrating hour spent setting the thing up, he finally gets it working, sticks the sucking teat onto the end of his cock and switches it to the highest setting. He quickly experiences an explosive orgasm, but

when it's all over he finds
he can't disengage from the
machine. Panicking, he dials
the customer service number
on the packaging and says,
'Hello, I have just purchased
one of your milking machines.
It all seems to be in working
order, but I can't seem to find
the release mechanism…'
'Not to worry Sir,' comes
the reply. 'The machine will
automatically disengage once
it has extracted two gallons.'

If I had a pet rooster,
you had a pet donkey,
and your donkey
ate my rooster, what
would you have?

My cock in your ass.

'Heello, I boouugghht aaaa vviibbrrattorr ffrroomm yourrrrr sshhopppp a fffffew daaays aggggooo.'
'Oh yes, how can I help?' 'Ccaann yyoouu tteell mmee hhooww ttoo ttuurrnn tthhee ffuucckkiinngg tthhiinngg ooffff?'

Sarah was comforting her 99-year-old grandmother after the death of her grandfather, and asked how he had died. Sobbing, her grandmother replied, 'He had a heart attack while we were making love last Sunday.' Shocked, Sarah said, 'Goodness, Granny! Having sex at your age, weren't you just asking for trouble?' 'No, no, darling,' said the grandmother, 'when we both started getting on a bit, we decided only

ever to make love when the
church bells were ringing
— that way we could keep to a
nice steady rhythm. You know:
in on the "Ding", out on the
"Dong"... and if wasn't for
that bloody ice cream truck,
he'd still be alive today!'

What three words
would you least like to
hear whilst having sex?

Honey, I'm home.

Two little boys are sitting next to each other in Sunday school. One little boy says to the other, 'Which part of the body goes to heaven first?' His friend replies, 'Oh, it's definitely the legs.' 'How do you know that?' asks the first boy. 'Well,' says the second boy, 'I've seen mummy on her back, waving her legs in the air and screaming, "Oh God, I'm coming!"'

A newly-wed deaf couple discover they're having some trouble communicating in bed once the lights go out, as it means they can't use sign language. After a few nights of frustrated fumblings, the wife comes up with an idea. 'Why don't we agree on some simple signals?' she signs. 'If you want to have sex with me, reach over and squeeze my left breast once. If you don't want to have sex, reach over and squeeze my right breast once.' The husband nods in approval and signs back to his wife, 'You're a genius! Likewise, if you want to have sex with me, reach over and pull on my penis once, but if you don't, just pull on it fifty times...'

How do you make a woman scream twice in the bedroom?

Once by making love to her and once by wiping yourself on her curtains.

Three blokes went on a camping holiday together and were sharing a tent. After their first night, the man on the right-hand side of the tent said, 'I had a really vivid dream last night, that a sexy girl was tossing me off.' 'That's weird,' said the man on the left-hand side of the tent, 'I dreamt the same thing.' The man in the middle sat up in bed and said, 'Sounds better than my dream — I dreamt I went skiing…'

A man walks into a bar and says 'C-c-can I h-have a b-b-beer?' The bartender replies, 'Of course. You know, I used to stutter myself, but one afternoon my wife gave me three blow-jobs in a row, and I haven't stuttered since!' The man says, 'Th-th-hanks, th-th-that's g-g-great adv-v-v-v-ice...' A week later, the man returns and once again asks, 'C-c-can I h-have a b-b-beer?' Curious, the bartender asks whether the man tried his stutter cure. 'Oh, I d-d-did!' says the man, 'It j-j-just d-d-didn't w-w-work. B-b-but I m-m-must say, your w-w-ife g-gives g-g-g-gr-great h-h-head!'

What do a homosexual
and a bungee jumper
have in common?

If the rubber breaks,
they're screwed.

A married couple who are having problems decide to go for counselling. The marriage counsellor turns to the wife first and asks what her main grievance is. 'The thing is,' she says, 'my husband suffers from premature ejaculation.' The counsellor asks the husband whether this is true. 'Well, no,' replies her husband, 'I don't suffer from it — but she does!'

A man who wants to lose weight goes to a diet centre. He is offered two treatments: one for £300 and another for £600. He chooses the cheapest option and a coach leads him to an athletics track where a former Olympic runner is set in front of him. She is absolutely stunning and completely naked but for a placard on her back saying, 'IF YOU CATCH ME, YOU GET TO SHAG ME'. They set off round the track and although he can't

catch her, he loses a couple
of pounds. A week later he
returns and requests the £600
treatment. 'Well, strip off and
get running. You can have a five
minute head start,' the coach
explains. Just as the man is
about to start running he spots
a hairy 25-stone giant wearing
a placard that reads, 'IF I CATCH
YOU, I GET TO SHAG YOU.'

A young man goes into a pub and orders a whisky. The barman serves him and the young man knocks it back in one. Surprised, the barman asks the young man if he's alright. The young man replies, 'It was my first-ever blowjob…' 'Ah,' smiles the barman, 'that's a big step in a man's life… have another whisky on the house to celebrate!' 'No thanks,' answers the young man. 'I'm alright now: that whisky got rid of the taste.'

What do you call a
female peacock?

A peacunt.

A man sees a sign outside
a bar that reads '£10 for a
good time'. Unable to resist
this offer, he goes in and pays
up. The bartender leads the
man to a back room where
he finds himself alone with a
sheep. Thinking he might as
well get his money's worth,
he has his way with the sheep
and leaves. The next week he
returns and this time sees a
sign which boasts, '£20 for the
time of your life!' He pays up,

but this time is taken upstairs to another room, where he finds a group of men staring through a crack in the floor. He peeks through and sees two people having sex. Impressed, he turns and gives the thumbs up to the bloke next to him, who says, 'Last week was even better; some pervert was shagging a sheep!'

A rugby player is lying in hospital after a debilitating kick to the groin. 'Are my testicles black?' he mumbles to the nurse through his oxygen mask. She raises his gown, cups his penis in one hand, feels his balls with the other and takes a close look. After her inspection she says, 'They seem to be fine.' The man removes his mask and says, 'Well, thanks for that — it was quite something! But what I really wanted to know is... ARE MY TEST RESULTS BACK?'

What's the first word
a test-tube baby
says to his father?

'Wanker!'

Three female flatmates had all been out on dates one night, and had arrived back home around the same time. The blonde said to the others, 'The sign of a good date is coming home with your hair in a mess.' The brunette said, 'No, the sign of a good date is coming home with your lipstick smudged across your face.' Without saying a word, the redhead pulled off her panties and flung them at the ceiling, where they

REALLY **dirty** JOKES

got stuck. 'Now THAT'S the sign
of a good date!' she said.

A man gets into a lift and
finds himself alone with a
beautiful woman. After a short
time he looks her way and
asks, 'Excuse me for asking,
but can I smell your fanny?'
Disgusted and indignant, the
woman replies, 'You certainly
cannot!' 'Oh,' says the man,
'it must be your feet then.'

Why are sperms
shaped like tadpoles?

Because frogs are
too hard to swallow.

A little old lady is late for mass and settles into a pew just as the priest is saying, '... and everyone who has recently committed adultery should stand up.' Being somewhat hard of hearing, she asks her neighbour to repeat what the priest has just said. 'He said everyone who wants a mint should stand up.' The old lady unsteadily gets to her feet, much to the priest's horror. He exclaims,

'At your age? You should be ashamed!' The old lady swiftly retorts, 'Just because I don't have any teeth left, doesn't mean I can't suck on something from time to time!'

A man walks into a pharmacy
and asks for some Viagra.
'I'm afraid I can't give you that
without a prescription,' says the
pharmacist. 'Do you have one?'
'No,' says the man, 'but take a
look at this photo of my wife...'

What happens when a
midget runs through
a woman's legs?

He gets a clit around
the ear and a flap
across the face.

Three novices were taking the final chastity test to join the priesthood. The bishop asked them to undress and gave each a small bell to attach to their penis. A beautiful girl entered the room and began stripping. As her bra came off, the first novice's bell rang with a loud 'Ting-a-ling!' The bishop told him he'd failed and sent him out for a cold shower. The girl continued her striptease, but as her pants came off a

'Ting-a-ling!' came from the
second novice's bell. He too
was sent out. By now the girl
was completely naked and
dancing in front of the third
novice, but not a sound was
heard. Satisfied, the bishop
said, 'I'm very proud of you.
You have shown the self-control
required to become a priest.
You may go and join your
companions for a shower and...'
The bishop was interrupted
by a loud 'Ting-a-ling!'

One night a man decides he wants to try something kinky and asks his wife if he can come in her ear. Outraged by this request, she refuses, adding that it could make her go deaf. 'Then why is it,' the man asks, 'that even though I've been coming in your mouth for the last twenty years, you're still fucking talking?'

Which animal can
change sex in less
than one second?

The crab.

dirty

JOKES

A man goes to his local for a
pint and finds one of his work
mates slouched at the bar. He
sits down next to him and asks
what the matter is. 'Well,' says
his friend, 'you know that girl
from work I've been wanting
to ask out? The one who
gives me an erection every
time I see her?' 'Oh you mean
Sharon from accounts?' replies
the first man. 'Yes, her. Well, I
finally asked her out by e-mail
and she accepted...' 'That's

great! When's the date?' asks
his friend. 'It was tonight, an
hour ago. I went to pick her up,
but as I was afraid of having
an erection in front of her I
sellotaped my prick to my leg,
just in case. When I got to hers,
she opened the door, wearing
an extra mini skirt and a low-cut
top...' 'So, what happened?' 'I
shoved my foot in her mouth.'

There are two whores in a lift. One whore says to the other whore. 'It smells of sperm in here.' The other whore replies, 'Oh, sorry! I just burped.'

A stunning woman is house-sitting for friends and decides to take a bath. As she slips into the water, the doorbell rings, but she can't find a towel so she calls out, 'Who's there?' and hears the response, 'It's the blind man.' Thinking that's rather lucky, she opens the door without bothering to cover herself up. 'Great boobs, love,' says the man. 'Now, where are those broken blinds?'

dirty
JOKES

Two teenagers are making
out. The girl asks the boy if
he wants to try a 69. 'What's
that?' asks the boy. 'Well,' the
girl explains, 'I put my head
between your legs while you put
yours between mine.' Without
fully understanding what she
means, but not wanting to
spoil his chances, the boy
agrees and they undress. Just
as they get into position, the
girl farts. The boy struggles
free and jumps off the bed in

disgust. The girl, embarrassed, apologises and promises it won't happen again. They move into position again, but straight away the girl lets out another stinker. Utterly revolted, the boy leaps up and begins to dress. 'What's going on? You're not leaving, are you?' asks the girl. The boy replies, 'Do you really think I'm going to hang around for the other 67?'

What's blue and
spits sawdust?

Smurfette after she's
given Pinocchio
a blow job.

Two cowboys were sitting in a bar, talking about sex. 'Hey,' says one cowboy to the other, 'have you tried the rodeo position?' 'No,' says the other cowboy, 'What's that?' His friend replies, 'Well you mount your wife from behind, reach around and cup her breasts in your hands. Then you say, "Boy, these are almost as nice as your sister's" and see how long you can hold on for.

A man on a train is eating
prawns, throwing the shells out
of the window. An old lady sat
opposite him says, 'Could you
stop doing that please? It's
disgusting!' He replies, 'Listen
Darling, I've paid for my ticket
so I'll do what I want on this
train!' and continues eating his
prawns. Once he's finished he
settles down for some shut-eye.
Meanwhile, the lady gets her
knitting out. Kept awake by the
incessant clinking, the man sits

up and says, 'Hey Granny! Can you stop that noise? I'm trying to sleep!' 'Listen Sweetie,' she replies, 'I also paid for my ticket and I'll do what I want!' Livid, the man stands up, grabs the needles and chucks them out the window. The old lady gets up and pulls the alarm signal. He laughs at her, 'You will get a fine for that!' She sneers back at him, 'And YOU will get ten years when the police smell your fingers!'

Why don't Essex girls
talk during sex?

Because mummy
always said not to
talk to strangers.

A man has just checked into a hotel for the night. As he turns away from the front desk, he bumps into the woman who is next in line and accidentally elbows her in the boob. The man immediately apologises profusely, then, noticing that she is very attractive, adds, 'If your heart is as soft as your breast, you'll forgive me.' She whispers back to him, 'If your cock's as hard as your elbow, I'm in room 436.'

A man enters a pharmacy,
buys a packet of condoms
and leaves the shop laughing
hysterically. The pharmacist
finds this a bit strange but
shrugs it off — after all, the
guy may be a bit disturbed,
but there's no law to prevent
disturbed people from buying
condoms. The next day the
man comes back, buys another
packet of condoms and leaves
the pharmacy in hysterics once
again. Intrigued, the pharmacis

calls his assistant over and says to him, 'If that bloke ever comes back, I want you to follow him to see where he goes.' Sure enough, on the following day he's back and repeats the performance. This time, the assistant follows him. An hour later, the assistant returns. 'So! What was he doing?' the pharmacist asks. 'Uh, well...' the assistant hesitates. 'I followed him to your house...'

Two mates were out for a pint
and the conversation soon
turned to sex. 'So, do you ever
do it doggy style with your
girlfriend?' said one to another.
'Not really,' his friend replied,
'I'd say she's more into dog
tricks than doggy style.' 'Oh,
so she's pretty kinky then?'
asked the first man, winking.
'Well, not exactly,' explained his
friend. 'I sit up and beg and
she rolls over and plays dead!'

REALLY
dirty
JOKES

What do westerns
and blue movies
have in common?

The heroes never
need to reload.

A man goes to the doctor's
complaining of an intense
stomach ache. The doctor
tells him he has a very serious
condition and prescribes a
suppository, which must be
inserted as deeply as possible.
The doctor warns him that it
will be painful and asks him
to bend over before pushing
the suppository deep into the
man's anus. He prescribes
a second dose of the drug
to take six hours later. At

home the man tries to insert the second suppository but struggles to reach the required depth. He calls his wife for help. She puts her hand on his shoulder to stabilise him and pushes the suppository in with her other hand. Suddenly the man shouts out, 'Bastard!' 'Did I hurt you?' asks his wife. 'No,' replies the man, 'but I've just realised that when the doctor put the first one in, BOTH his hands were on my shoulders!'

A man walks into a pub and starts downing shot after shot of whisky. Concerned, the landlord asks if he's alright. 'Not really,' sighs the man. 'I just found my wife in bed with my best friend.' 'Oh dear,' says the landlord, 'What did you say to her?' The man shakes his head and says 'Nothing'. 'So what did you say to your best friend?' The man replies, 'I said "Bad dog! VERY bad dog!"'

REALLY dirty JOKES

What do cars
and blokes have
in common?

Both misfire.

One day Jane decided to give Tarzan some sex education. 'Look Tarzan, the thing you have between your legs is like your laundry. And what is between my own legs, is like a washing machine... So, all you have to do is put your laundry into my washing machine and squeeze it well before taking it out.' For the five following nights, Tarzan did the washing non-stop. When he finally stopped for a break, Jane said to him, 'Listen, Tarzan, you can't keep doing the laundry constantly — you're going to wear out my washing machine! You'll have to wait for two or three days before doing your next load.' Tarzan was very disappointed at this. After a month of no laundry, Jane asked him: 'Tarzan, what's wrong with you? Why haven't you put your laundry into my machine for a month?' Tarzan replied: 'Tarzan handwash!'

A man is roaming the red-light district when an attractive prostitute approaches him and invites him back to her room. Once there, she undresses and lies on the bed. The man just stares at her, and after a while she asks, 'What's wrong? Is this the first time you've seen a pussy since you came out of one?' The man replies, 'No, but it's the first one I've seen that's big enough for me to get back into.'

What do men do both
in the car and in bed?

Pull out before
checking to see if
anyone else is coming.

At a tribal coming of age
ceremony, a youth is placed in
front of three tents. The chief
of the tribe says to him, 'In the
first tent there is a barrel of
plum wine: you must drink it all.
In the second tent there is a
puma with a raging toothache:
you must take out the bad
tooth. And in the third tent
awaits a woman who has never
had an orgasm...' The young
Indian enters the first tent and
comes back out of it rather

quickly, holding the empty barrel and looking somewhat worse for the wear. The tribe applauds him. He bumbles into the second tent. The tribe holds its breath as terrible screams, yowls and growls issue forth from the tent. Just when everyone begins to think the young man must be dead he emerges, exhausted and bloody, and says, 'Now lead me to the woman with the toothache!'

Lisa meets up with her friend Jackie for a night of revelry at their local nightclub. Lisa is shocked by the belt-like proportions of Jackie's skirt and says so. 'And that's not all...' says Jackie with a mischievous wink as she lifts her mini-skirt. 'No pants? That's a bit kinky isn't it?' says Lisa. 'So what?' says Jackie. 'When you go to a concert you don't put earplugs in!'

Why do men find
inspiration in bed?

Because that's when
they're plugged
into a genius.

The Queen was visiting a hospital where several new wards had opened. On her guided tour of the hospital, she hears orgasmic moans coming from a room down the corridor. Overcome with curiosity, she slips away and goes into the room to investigate. There she finds a man is openly masturbating on the bed. She calls to a nurse and asks why he's doing that and the nurse replies, 'He suffers from a rare condition which makes him nee

to relieve himself regularly.'
Slightly revolted but determined
not to appear fazed, the Queen
continues her tour, only to hear
more orgasmic noises from
another room further along.
This time she goes into the
room to find a nurse giving a
patient a blow job. Somewhat
alarmed, she asks her escort
what's going on. The nurse
replies, 'This man has the same
disorder as the man you saw
in the previous room, but this
one has health insurance.'

Two 90-year-olds had been dating for a while when the man said to the woman, 'Well, tonight's the night we have sex!' And so they did. As they lay next to each other in bed afterwards, the man turned to the woman and said, 'If I'd known you were a virgin, I'd have been much more gentle.' The woman replied, 'Well if I'd known you'd actually manage to get it up, I'd have taken my knickers off!'

What do a hard
penis and a bone
have in common?

There are always
bitches running
after them.

A man returns home after a hard day's work to find his wife on all fours on the kitchen floor, scraping out the tiling. The sight of her wobbling bottom excites him and he takes her there and then. As soon as it's over he calls her a bitch. The woman is outraged and cries out, 'For God's sake, what's wrong with you? I satisfy your fantasy by letting you take me by surprise without the least objection, and all you

REALLY **dirty** JOKES

can do is be rude to me?' The husband looks at her angrily and replies, 'You didn't even look back to see who it was!'

A cucumber is chatting to an olive and a penis and says to them, 'My life is so depressing. When I get big, fat and juicy they're going to slice me up and put me in salad.' The olive says, 'It's worse for me: when I get big, fat and juicy they'll chop me into bits and sprinkle me on a pizza.' The penis says, 'I can top that! When I get big, fat and juicy, they stick a bag over my head, shove me down a narrow tunnel and leave me there till I throw up.'

What do a woman
and a coffin have
in common?

You can only get into
them once you're stiff.

A wife tells her husband that she dreamt she went to a dick auction, where the big ones were going for £10 and the thick ones were selling for £20. The husband asked her, 'And what about the ones like mine?' To which she replied, 'Oh, they were just giving those away.' The husband then described his dream, in which he was at a pussy auction where the pretty ones were going for £100 and the tight ones were going for

£200. 'How much were people paying for ones like mine?' asked the wife. 'Oh,' says the husband, 'That's where they were holding the auction.'

What do women have in common with fried chicken?

When you've had your fill of legs and breast, you've got a nice greasy box to stick your bone in.

Why is an umbrella
like a cock?

You have to get it up to
use it, it comes down
when you're done and
dribbles after use.

Two ducks go away together for a dirty weekend. However, when they arrive in their hotel room, they realise they've forgotten to bring any condoms, so the male duck calls room service and asks for one to be sent up. Moments later, there's a knock at the door. The male duck opens the door to a find a man with a condom on a tray. He takes the condom, puts a tip on the tray and says thank you. Before he leaves the

man asks, 'Sir, would you like
me to put that on your bill?'
'Good lord no!' quacks the
duck in shock. 'Do you think
I'm some sort of pervert?!'

REALLY
dirty
JOKES

A really tall man is getting married to a very short woman. At
the wedding reception, his best
man can't resist asking, 'So,
how do you two manage to have
sex?' To which his tall friend
replies, 'Well, I sit on a chair, she
gets on top, I grab her waist
and bob her up and down. It's a
bit like wanking really, only with
someone to talk to.'

What's the difference between a catholic priest and acne?

Acne only comes on a boy's face after he turns 12.

Three old men were sitting
on a park bench and talking
about the difficulties of old
age. The first old man said to
the others, 'You know, these
days my hands shake so
badly, that when I had a shave
this morning, I cut myself.'
The second old man said, 'I
know what you mean — mine
were shaking so much when
I mowed the lawn yesterday
that I cropped all my flowers!'
'It's not all bad,' said the

third old man with a chuckle. 'My hands shake so much that when I went for a piss yesterday, I came three times!'

A couple are celebrating their twenty-fifth wedding anniversary and have returned to the hotel where they spent their honeymoon. As they reminisce about their first night together, the wife asks the husband, 'Darling, what were you thinking the first time you saw me standing naked in front of you?' The husband replies, 'I was just thinking how much I wanted to shag your brains out, and suck

your tits dry.' Feeling horny,
the wife begins to undress
and asks cheekily, 'And what
are you thinking right now?'
Surveying her body he replies,
'I'm thinking that it looks as
if I did a pretty good job.'

Why did the farmer cross the road?

Because his dick was stuck up the chicken.

Why is a dirty
slapper better than
a bowling ball?

You can only get
three fingers into
a bowling ball.

Two golfers meet on the course, fall in love and get married. On their honeymoon night, they make love for the first time. Afterwards, the man picks up the phone and starts dialling. 'Who are you calling?' asks the bride. 'Room service,' her husband replies. 'I'm starving.' 'Tiger Woods wouldn't do that,' she says, 'he would make love to me again!' So they make love again. When they're done, the husband picks up the phone. 'You aren't calling room service, are you?' she asks plaintively. 'You know, Tiger Woods wouldn't do that. He would make love to me again.' The man sighs a bit and proceeds to make love to his new wife one more time. All of his energy spent, he struggles to pick up the phone. 'Are you calling room service?' she smiles. 'Am I hell! I'm calling Tiger Woods to find out what the par is on this bloody hole!'

A man had always dreamt of having a pair of real cowboy boots. One day he sees a pair on sale, decides to treat himself and walks proudly back home in his new boots. He enters the house and asks his wife, 'Do you notice anything different about me?' The wife looks him up and down and says that she doesn't. Frustrated, the husband locks himself in the bathroom, takes off his clothes and comes back completely naked but still wearing his cowboy boots. He asks his wife, 'And NOW do you notice something different?' The wife looks at him again and says, 'What's different darling? It droops today, drooped yesterday and it will still be drooping tomorrow...' Furious, the husband cries out, 'And do you know why? It's drooping because it's admiring my new cowboy boots! So maybe you should buy a new hat!'

What do a woman
and a frying pan
have in common?

Both need warming
up before you put
the meat in.

A man sees a female colleague in the staff room and tells her that her hair smells nice. The woman gets furious and immediately storms into the boss's office. 'I want to lodge a complaint for sexual harassment!' she shouts out, and proceeds to describe the incident. The boss replies, 'But what's wrong with that? A colleague tells you that your hair smells nice and you want to lodge a complaint?' She replies, 'He's a midget!'

A couple head back to the man's flat after a date. As the man gets his key out the woman says, 'Did you know you can judge a lover by the way he unlocks a door?' 'Is that true? How?' asks the man. 'Well,' says the woman, 'For example, if a man sticks the key straight in and barges through the door, that means he's rough in bed, which I don't like. And if it takes him ages to get the key in the slot, he's inexperienced, which I don't like either.' Then she asks him, 'So, what's your approach?' The man replies, 'Well, before I even try to put my key in, I give the lock a good licking.'

What do you call
Bill Clinton's fly?

The US Open.

Two old drunks are in a pub talking about the good old days. One says to the other, 'I can still recall the first time I resorted to alcohol for want of a woman.' 'Really? So, what happened?' asks his fellow drinker. The first drunk replies, 'It was pretty good, but I had a hell of a job getting my cock out of the bottle afterwards.'

What's green and slimy
and smells of pork?

Kermit's finger.

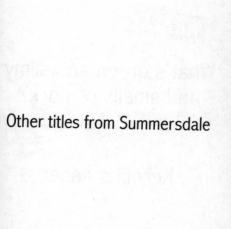

Other titles from Summersdale

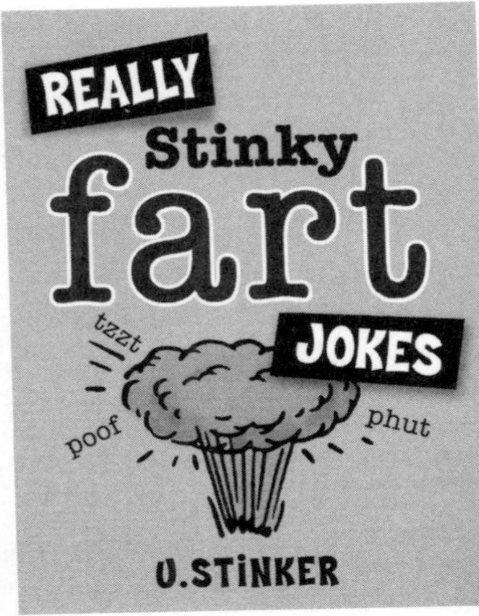
REALLY
Stinky
fart
JOKES
tzzt
poof
phut
U.STINKER

REALLY STINKY FART JOKES

U. STINKER

£2.99

Paperback

'Did you here about the blind skunk?
He's dating a fart.'

There's no denying it – flatulence is funny. Bath bubblers, duvet fluffers and follow-throughs: this pungent little book has a joke for every farting occasion.

One whiff of these little stinkers will have you gagging for more.

REALLY

sick

JOKES

G. ROOSOM